licensed, or endorsed by the aforementioned interests or any of their licensees.

About the Publisher
Epiphany Printing is a member of the **BLVNP Incorporated Group,**
340 S. Lemon #6200, Walnut, CA 91789, info@blvnp.com /
legal@blvnp.com

I0116180

TRUMP VS. CLINTON

Facts and Trivia on America's Most Heated Presidential Rivalry

By Bern Bolo

© **Bern Bolo 2016**
ISBN: 978-1-68030-711-5

TABLE OF CONTENTS

***

FREE DOWNLOAD

CLINTON'S COMEBACK

The Weird and interesting **secrets** of **Hillary Clinton**

Learn all about Hillary in 20 minutes

With Bern Bolo
The Bathroom Genius

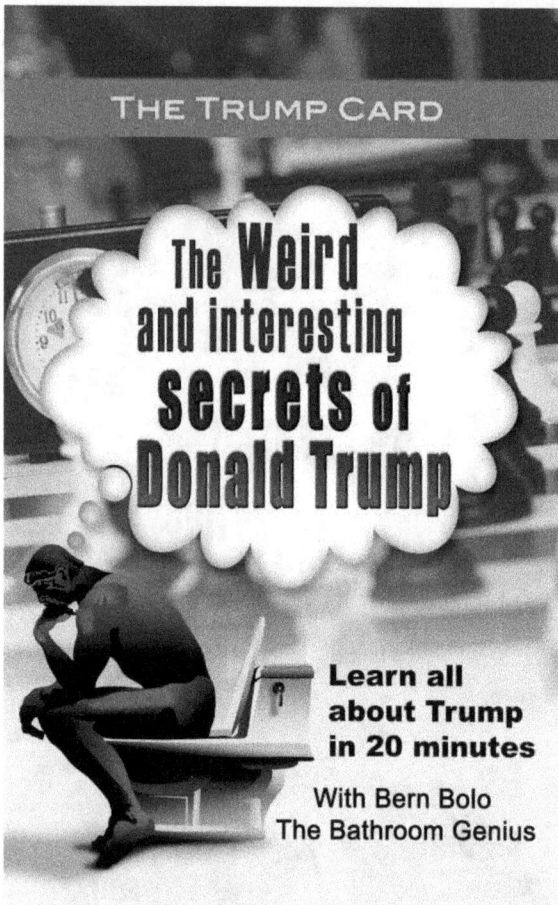

THE TRUMP CARD

The **Weird** and interesting **secrets** of **Donald Trump**

Learn all about Trump in 20 minutes

With Bern Bolo
The Bathroom Genius

Know more about **CLINTON'S COMEBACK and THE TRUMP CARD**
by reading the **FREE Chapters** when you sign up for my mailing list!

bern-bolo.awesomeauthors.org

TRUMP VERSUS CLINTON:

A HEATED RIVALRY FOR PRESIDENCY

"I try to learn from the past,
but I plan for the future by focusing
exclusively on the present.
That's where the fun is."
* - Donald Trump*

"Every moment wasted looking back,
keeps us from moving forward."

* - Hillary Clinton*

The Rivalry Heat Is On!

Donald Trump and Hillary Clinton are definitely opposites of each other. Their attitudes, approaches and accomplishments show how different they really are all throughout their lives. One thing is common though between two – they are out to get what they truly want for themselves. Donald Trump is sure to get results in business and leadership while Hillary Clinton has great experience in law and politics. It would be nice if we have a president who characterizes the best of both worlds, but if you were to choose the next president of the United States of America, who would it be?

This Trivia book has information which will tide you over the entire period before the upcoming elections. Here we discuss the characteristics and accomplishments of these two high-profile presidential candidates. This book might also help you determine the candidate you would bet your life on for the next four or eight years.

The first two chapters will take you to a comparison of the personal and professional lives of both candidates to give you an idea of their early endeavors and help you get to know the type of experiences that shaped them.

Then, the next chapter will introduce their specific standpoint on issues and even contain direct quotes from Donald and Hillary. Find out what they stand for to help you discern which candidate you want to vote for next election.

So hold on to your seat and do not forget to breathe. The heat is on between the business mogul and the political power woman to decide America's future!

TRUMP VERSUS CLINTON: PERSONAL LIVES

"As long as you are going to be thinking anyway, think big."

Donald Trump

"Fail to plan, plan to fail."

-   Hillary Clinton

FAST FACTS ABOUT HILLARY AND DONALD

Get to know these two president-hopefuls. Hillary is more than just a veteran in American politics, and Donald is more than an opinionated business mogul.

	HILLARY DIANE RODHAM CLINTON	**DONALD JOHN TRUMP**
Born	October 26, 1947	June 14, 1946
Birthplace	Chicago, Illinois	Queens, New York City
Parents	Father – Hugh Rodham, Mother – Dorothy Emma	Father – Fred Trump Mother – Mary Anne MacLeod
	Hillary is the eldest of three children	Donald is the fourth among five children
Occupation	US Secretary of State (2009 – 2013)	Chairman and President of The Trump Organization
	Senator from the State of New York (2001 – 2009)	Chairman of Trump Plaza Associates, LLC

	United States First Lady (1993 – 2001)	Chairman of Trump Atlantic City Associates
	First Lady of Arkansas (1983 – 1992)	Founder of Trump Entertainment Resorts
Children	Chelsea	Donald Trump Jr., Ivanka, Eric, Tiffany, Barron
Grandchildren	Charlotte	Joseph Frederick Kushner, Arabella Rose Kushner, Kai Madison Trump, Tristan Milos Trump, Donald Trump III, Chloe Sophia Trump, Spencer Frederick Trump
Residence	Chappaqua, New York	Manhattan, New York
Religion	Presbyterian	Methodist

Political Party	Democrat	Republican

EARLY LIFE

HILLARY DIANE RODHAM CLINTON	DONALD JOHN TRUMP
Born from a middle-class family with a father in the textile business and homemaker mother	Born from a rich family with successful real estate developer as a father and a philanthropist mother
Active in sports and activities in primary school and proceeded to graduate as a National Merit Finalist belonging to the top 5% of her class.	Energetic and assertive as a child but was able to channel his energy to become a student leader and a top athlete when he went to military school.
The first student to graduate from Wellesley College to deliver a commencement speech, receiving a seven-minute standing ovation.	Worth, at least, $200,000 when he graduated from Wharton School of Business.
First worked as a staff attorney at Children's	Began his business career in his father's real estate company and

Defense Fund.	expanded the business
Rumored to have tried entering the Marines but was not accepted.	Was, at first, eligible to be drafted to the Vietnam War but was medically disqualified due to heel spurs

LOVE LIFE

HILLARY DIANE RODHAM CLINTON	DONALD JOHN TRUMP
Met Bill as a fellow student at Yale Law School and refused Bill's proposal of marriage as she was unsure if she wanted to tie her future with his but finally agreed to the wedding by 1975	Married the model Ivana Zelníčková on 1977 and had three children but divorced on 1991 due to his affair with actress Marla Maples
Used her own last name to the chagrin of their mothers until 1982, when she started using Clinton	Had a child from Marla Maples and married her two months later but they separated in 1997 and divorced last 1999
Bill's affair with actress Monica	Remarried to the model

Lewinsky caused problems and led to the impeachment of Bill, but the couple stayed married.

Melania Knauss last 2005 and had another child with her

TRUMP VERSUS CLINTON: PROFESSIONAL ENDEAVORS

"I want to win for the people of this great country. The only people I will owe are the voters. The media, special interests, and lobbyists are all trying to stop me. We won't let that happen!"

- *Donald Trump*

"I will work harder than anyone to actually make change that makes your life better."
- *Hillary Clinton*

PROFESSIONAL LIVES

Both talented in their own right, Hillary, and Donald have become leading figures in their chosen discipline. See the journey that has led them to the race for the 2016 elections.

EDUCATION

	HILLARY DIANE RODHAM CLINTON	DONALD JOHN TRUMP
Primary	Eugene Field Elementary School	Kew-Forest School
Secondary	Maine South High School Maine East High School	New York Military Academy
Tertiary	Wellesley College: BA in Political Science Yale Law School: Juris Degree in Law	Fordham University Wharton School of Business – University of Pennsylvania: BS in Economics

OCCUPATION HISTORY

HILLARY DIANE RODHAM CLINTON

DONALD JOHN TRUMP

She became a member of the impeachment inquiry staff of President Richard Nixon last 1974.

By 1971, he gained control of the company and renamed it to Trump Organization and became involved in large building projects in Manhattan.

Became a faculty member at the University of Arkansas Law School in Fayetteville

Opened the Grand Hyatt Hotel in 1980, making him one of New York's most successful developer.

Joined the Rose Law Firm and cofounded Arkansas Advocates for Children and Families by 1977.

Opened the $ 200-million apartment-retail complex, Trump Tower, on Fifth Avenue last 1982.

As First Lady of Arkansas for four terms, she was involved with the Rural Health Advisory Committee, Arkansas Education Standards Committee, Arkansas Children's Hospital, Arkansas Legal Services and the Children's Defense Fund.

Entered the casino business and bought an apartment building which faced Central Park, renovated Barbizon and named it Trump Parc and acquired the Plaza Hotel but the 76 acres he bought on the West Side of Manhattan where Television City was supposed to be built was faced with intense opposition.

19

First Lady of the US and headed the Task Force on National Health Reform. She also promoted children and women's rights and healthcare and traveled to several parts of the world, playing a role in US diplomacy.

Expanded in the south, developing both commercial and residential areas. The decline of the real estate market posed problems for a while, but he was able to bounce back.

Became the first wife of a president to seek and win a public office and the first woman in US Senate from New York and won the reelection.

Real estate expanded to golf courses and resorts and invested in other ventures, mostly in the financial market, but also in sports, beauty pageants and entertainment.

Announced candidacy for president but lost the 2008 Democratic Party nomination to Barrack Obama.

Thought about running for the presidency during 1988, 2004 and 2012 and as Governor of New York but did not pursue the thought.

Became the first wife of a former president to become the US Secretary of State.

Continued building construction and began a reality series on NBC called *The Apprentice.*

Announced her candidacy via a YouTube clip.

Announced candidacy at the Trump Towers in New York City.

ACCOMPLISHMENTS

HILLARY DIANE RODHAM CLINTON

fter Eleanor Roosevelt, she is garded as one of the <u>most</u> <u>benly empowered</u> esidential wives in American story and the most widely aveled, visiting 79 countries.

ecame the first First Lady to e elected to public office and e first female senator from e state of New York where e sponsored three laws and sponsored seventy-four.

nly former First Lady to be ominated and to serve as the ecretary of State and is the ost traveled going to 112 ountries.

on a Grammy in 1997 for est Spoken Word Album for e audio version of her book, It Takes a Village."

DONALD JOHN TRUMP

Built the following buildings that established and made him famous in the Real Estate Business:

- Grand Hyatt Hotel
- New York's Wollman Rink
- Trump Tower

<u>Financial statement</u> declaring net worth in the billions of dollars and has 515 properties all over the world, with his last name appearing on 268 of them.

One of the highest paid personalities on television earning him a star on the Hollywood Walk of Fame.

Nominated for the Emmy twice (2004 and 2005) for Outstanding Reality-Competition Program for his TV show "*The Apprentice.*"

Among the top 100 most influential lawyers in America last 1988 and 1991 according to the National Law Journal.

Named as the Top Six among the most admired men and women alive according t a USA Today/Gallup poll.

CONTROVERSY INVOLVEMENT

HILLARY DIANE RODHAM CLINTON

As First Lady, she was investigated by the United State Office of the Independent Counsel due to:

- Whitewater Controversy – alleged that Bill Clinton pressured Susan McDougal to make a federally backed loan when he was still the governor of Arkansas.
- Travelgate – Hillary was alleged with falsifying statements and playing a big role in the firing of the employees.
- Filegate – Hillary and other leaders of the White House were alleged to have improperly requested and read confidential files of White House employees from a previous Republican administration.
- Cattle Futures Controversy – her cattle trading was accused of possible conflict of interest and disguised bribery.

The scandal of husband's affair,

DONALD JOHN TRUMP

Filed for corporate bankruptcy four times (although he has never declared personal bankruptcy) to repay the debts and restructure the organization:

- 1991 (Trump's Taj Mahal in Atlantic City) – gave up half of his share in the casino and sell his yacht and airline
- 1992 (Trump Plaza Hotel in Atlantic City) – gave up 49% to Citibank and other lenders but stayed CEO
- 2004 (Trump Hotels and Casinos Resort) – resulted to him giving up most of the control of the company
- 2009 (Trump Entertainment Resorts) – reduced his stake in the company further and even resigned as the head of the board

Divorce with his first wife has been

known as the Lewinsky scandal, led to the impeachment of Bill Clinton in the Congress. At first, she denied the allegation and said that it was a part of the "right-wing conspiracy" to oust Bill from the White House. When he admitted to the affair, she released a public statement about her commitment to the marriage. Privately, though, she was reported to be upset at him and unsure about their marriage.

controversial due to his alleged affair with actress, Marla Maples.

As Secretary of State, there were two issues that stood out:

- The 2012 Benghazi attacks resulted in the death of four Americans and questioned the security of the US diplomats when on a mission.
- Her usage of a personal private email for official business rather than the government one was revealed and the deletion of almost 32,000 emails she considered as private violated certain protocols and laws. This arose during March 2015 and was known as the Email Controversy.

Has filed lawsuits to:

- Forbes and another reporter for inaccurate statement of his net worth
- Miss USA contestant Sheena Monnin for posting on her Facebook page that the pageant was "fraudulent," "trashy," and "rigged."
- Bill Maher for not paying $5 million when the comedian offered said sum when Trump proves that his father is not an orangutan.

TRUMP VERSUS CLINTON: POLITICAL STANDPOINTS

"America has been great to me, I want to be great to America. I want to put us back on the right course and Make America Great Again!"

- *Donald Trump*

"Everyday Americans need a champion. And I want to be that champion."

- *Hillary Clinton*

POLITICAL STANDPOINT

Aside from being a Democrat or a Republican, what do these two candidates have in store for America? Find out where they stand on specific issues and what plans they have if they win as president.

HILLARY DIANE RODHAM CLINTON

"Every day Americans need a champion. And I want to be that champion."

She was in an elective office for eight years and 30 years in public office from the First Lady of Arkansas to being the Secretary of the State.

Raised as a Republican, her political affiliation started to change in college, and she became a Democrat from then on.

DONALD JOHN TRUMP

"Make America great again!"

No experience in politics but known to be critical and well-informed and has strong leadership qualities as shown in the handling of business

Started as a Democrat until 1987, when he changed to different parties before settling in the Republican since 2012.

CRIMES AND GUNS

"I do support comprehensive background checks, and to close the gun show loophole, and

"The right of self-defense doesn't stop at the end of your driveway.

the online loophole, and what's called the Charleston loophole, and to prevent people on the no-fly list from getting guns."

That's why I have a concealed carry permit and why tens of millions of Americans do too. That permit should be valid in all 50 states."

- Against stricter punishment for crimes

- Supports capital punishment
- Pro-gun control with a ban on assault rifles

- Promote stricter punishment as means of reducing crime
- Supports capital punishment
- Against gun ban

ECONOMY

"If you do your part, then you ought to be able to get ahead. You ought to be able to reap the rewards of your work. And when everybody does his or her part, then America gets ahead."

"I will bring jobs back from China, I will bring jobs back from Japan. I will bring jobs back from Mexico."

- Stimulus-led economy recovery, letting the federal government put funding to help the country recuperate
- Support raising the minimum wage

- Market-led recovery, keeping the federal government out of the economy and its recuperation
- Against raising

- Reestablish balanced budget and keep expenditures equal or below revenues
- Propose a tax reform which raises taxes on the wealthy and a tax relief on working families
- Sees national debt as an issue on US national security and will pay it using the budget surplus

- minimum wage
- Reestablish balanced budget and keep expenditures equal or below revenues
- Will simplify the tax code, raise tax on the wealthy and decrease tax on the middle class
- Plans to pay debts by cutting down government spending and increasing jobs

EDUCATION

"We need to make a quality education affordable and available to everyone willing to work for it, without saddling them with decades of debt."

"I'm a tremendous believer in education, but education has to be at a local level. We cannot have the bureaucrats in Washington telling you how to manage your child's education."

- Doesn't support using government-funded vouchers to be used in private schools
- Supports Common Core and No Child Left Behind program

- Promotes usage of government-funded vouchers for private school tuition
- Will keep education at the local level and oppose Common Core

ENVIRONMENT

"Climate change is real – no matter what climate deniers say."

"The concept of global warming was created by and for the Chinese in order to make US manufacturing non-competitive."

- Promote use of green energy
- EPA regulations are not restrictive
- Believes in climate change

- Will not prioritize green energy
- Cut the EPA as it's too restrictive
- Needs proof to believe in climate change

FOREIGN POLICY

"Israel has every reason to be alarmed by a regime that both denies its existence and seeks its destruction."

"A nation without borders is not a nation."

- Oppose free trade (open trade with every country) and replace it with

- Oppose free trade (open trade with every

fair trade
- Oppose American Exceptionalism and, instead, build alliances with other countries for mutual benefit
- Promote foreign entanglements and help Afghanistan defend itself
- Supports opening commerce with Cuba

country) and replace i with fair trade
- Support American Exceptionalism and not allow US forces to serve under other countries' command
- Avoid foreign entanglements and exi Iran, Iraq and Afghanistan
- Support opening commerce with Cuba

HEALTHCARE

"I won't cut Social Security. ... I'll defend it, and I'll expand it."

"I would end Obamacare and replace it with something terrific, for far less money for the country and the people."

- Will improve Obamacare

- Pro-choice and supports abortion

- Expand

- Replace Obamacare with Universal Health Care
- Pro-life and against abortion except during cases of health, incest or rape issues
- Agrees on privatizing of social security and

social security but against privatizing it

puts money on the program by taking back money being sent to other countries

HUMAN RIGHTS

Being LGBT does not make you less human. And that is why gay rights are human rights and human rights are gay rights."

"We want people to come into our country, but they have to come into our country legally."

- Strongly support Affirmative Action to proportionally represent women and minorities in the economy and workplace
- Provide illegal immigrants a path to citizenship
- Promotes same-sex marriage

- Facilitate easier voter registrations
- Disagrees in keeping God in the public

- Have government enforce the end to racial injustice rather than simply enforce Affirmative Action
- Wants to return criminal aliens but welcome legal foreigners
- Against same-sex marriage but accepts its legalization
- Facilitate easier voter registrations
- Wants to keep God in the public sphere

31

SECURITY AND TERRORISM

"Our goal is not to deter or contain ISIS, but to defeat and destroy ISIS."

"I would bomb the hell out of ISIS."

- Disagrees on expanding the military

- Engage ISIS on their home turf and work with allies to cut their network on ground and online

- Increase military spending to expand military
- Advocate targeting families of ISIS terrorist but will strive to minimize civilian casualties

VETERANS

"I believe in making sure that people who sacrifice for us are given all the care and the benefits and support that they need. And I believe strongly that taking care of our veterans is part of our solemn duty as Americans."

"The power to choose will stop the wait time backlogs and force the VA to improve and compete if the department wants to keep receiving veterans' healthcare dollars."

- Ensure to give veterans access to good education, good jobs, high-quality health care and family support

- Will upgrade Veteran Affairs facilities increasing funding for education, job training placement services and business loans for veterans and modernize Department of Veteran Affairs

To find out more about their platforms and their stands on issues, you can always check out their respective sites:
https://www.donaldjtrump.com/ and https://www.hillaryclinton.com/

TRUMP VERSUS CLINTON: WHO WILL PREVAIL?

"It will change. We will have so much winning if I get elected that you may get bored with winning. Believe me."

- *Donald Trump*

"I'm going to keep talking about tearing down all the barriers that stand in the way of Americans fulfilling their potential. I don't think our country can live up to its potential unless we give a chance to every single American to live up to theirs."

- *Hillary Clinton*

CONCLUSION
Who Might Win in the 2016 US Presidential Elections?

As of February 2016, Hillary Clinton is leading the polls for other presidential candidates. There are more experts who say that Hillary Clinton would be more likely to win the elections. However, Donald Trump is gaining momentum since he announced his candidacy. Still, it is imperative that both candidates win the nominations of their respective parties first.

If Hillary Clinton wins, there are going to be changes in politics and governance in different sectors of the society such as education and human rights. If Donald Trump wins, you will get to witness how a result-driven businessman will run the country and expect changes in national security and economy.

It might be too early to say who will bag the honor of becoming the next president of the United States, especially as they are still both campaigning to gain their party's nomination. Poll statistics might change at the very last minute. But isn't this the most thrilling time in US politics wherein the two most famous presidential candidates are known to be very good at what they do?

Whoever becomes the next President of America, you can expect ingenious initiatives and controversial issues. The vital thing is for you to exercise your right to suffrage and vote for the person who stands for the principles that you believe in.

Donald Trump and Hillary Clinton are two people on polar-opposites of the scale who are both trying to gain their respective party's nomination to carry out their interesting plans for the country. Different from each other in more ways than one, the election of either one in the office could prove to be an important turning point in American history.

REFERENCES

Personal and Professional

https://www.donaldjtrump.com/

https://www.hillaryclinton.com/

https://www.youtube.com/watch?v=q_q61B-DyPk

https://www.youtube.com/watch?v=0uY7gLZDmn4&feature=youtu.be

http://presidential-candidates.insidegov.com/compare/40-70/Hillary-Clinton-vs-Donald-Trump

http://2016.candidate-comparison.org/?compare=Clinton&vs=Trump

http://www.biography.com/people/donald-trump-9511238

http://www.encyclopedia.com/topic/Hillary_Rodham_Clinton.aspx

http://time.com/4231739/hillary-clinton-nevada-caucuses-texas/

http://fortune.com/2015/09/29/trump-forbes-net-worth/

http://www.theatlantic.com/national/archive/2013/03/the-lawsuits-of-donald-trump/273819/

http://www.fool.com/investing/general/2015/10/25/donald-trumps-5-biggest-successes.aspx

http://www.hrc.org/2016RepublicanFacts/donald-trump

https://www.congress.gov/member/hillary-clinton/C001041?q=%7B%22bill-status%22%3A%22law%22%7D

http://www.stockpickssystem.com/donald-trump/

https://www.documentcloud.org/documents/2175187-trump.html

https://www.govtrack.us/congress/members/hillary_clinton/300022

http://www.usatoday.com/story/news/politics/onpolitics/2015/12/28/obama-donald-trump-gallup-poll-most-admired-man/77967868/

https://en.wikipedia.org/wiki/Whitewater_controversy

https://en.wikipedia.org/wiki/White_House_travel_office_controversy

https://en.wikipedia.org/wiki/White_House_FBI_files_controversy

https://en.wikipedia.org/wiki/Hillary_Rodham_cattle_futures_controversy

https://en.wikipedia.org/wiki/Donald_Trump
https://en.wikipedia.org/wiki/Hillary_Clinton

Political

http://www.hrc.org/blog/five-of-hillary-clintons-best-quotes-on-lgbt-equality
http://www.kcci.com/politics/2-potential-candidates-visit-iowa-today/32253026
http://www.politico.com/story/2016/02/gop-debate-rubio-chris-christie-fight-218873
http://dailycaller.com/2016/01/26/trump-pledges-to-kill-common-core/
http://www.nytimes.com/interactive/2016/us/elections/candidates-on-the-issues.html?_r=0
http://www.ontheissues.org/Hillary_Clinton.htm
http://www.ontheissues.org/Donald_Trump.htm
http://www.postandcourier.com/article/20150721/PC1603/150729864/trump-gives-out-graham-x2019-s-cellphone-number-after-senator-calls-him-a-x2018-jackass-x2019
http://abcnews.go.com/Politics/donald-trump-outlines-plan-reform-veterans-affairs/story?id=34878656
http://edition.cnn.com/2015/10/03/politics/donald-trump-oregon-shooting-armed-teachers/
https://www.washingtonpost.com/news/post-politics/wp/2016/02/04/in-new-hampshire-trumps-pitch-is-urgent-and-his-schedule-packed/
http://www.nbcnews.com/politics/2016-election/sticking-resolution-clinton-has-nothing-say-trump-n490836
http://www.huffingtonpost.com/entry/hillary-clinton-iran-foreign-policy_us_55f05c2ae4b002d5c07786b2

Can't get enough of
CLINTON'S COMEBACK and THE TRUMP CARD?
Make sure you sign up for my blog to find out more..!

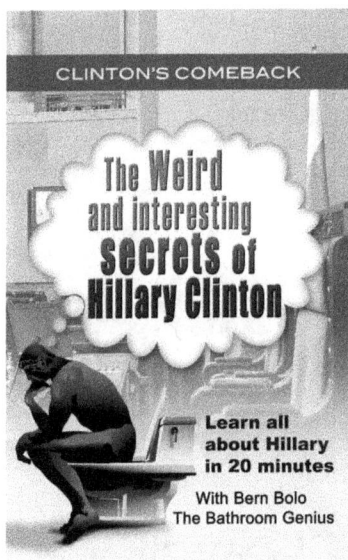

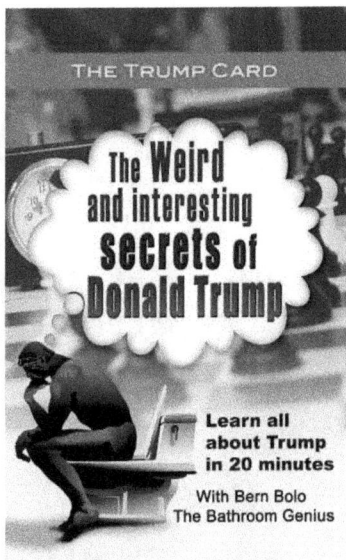

Get this **bonus chapters** when you sign up at <u>bern-bolo.awesomeauthors.org</u>

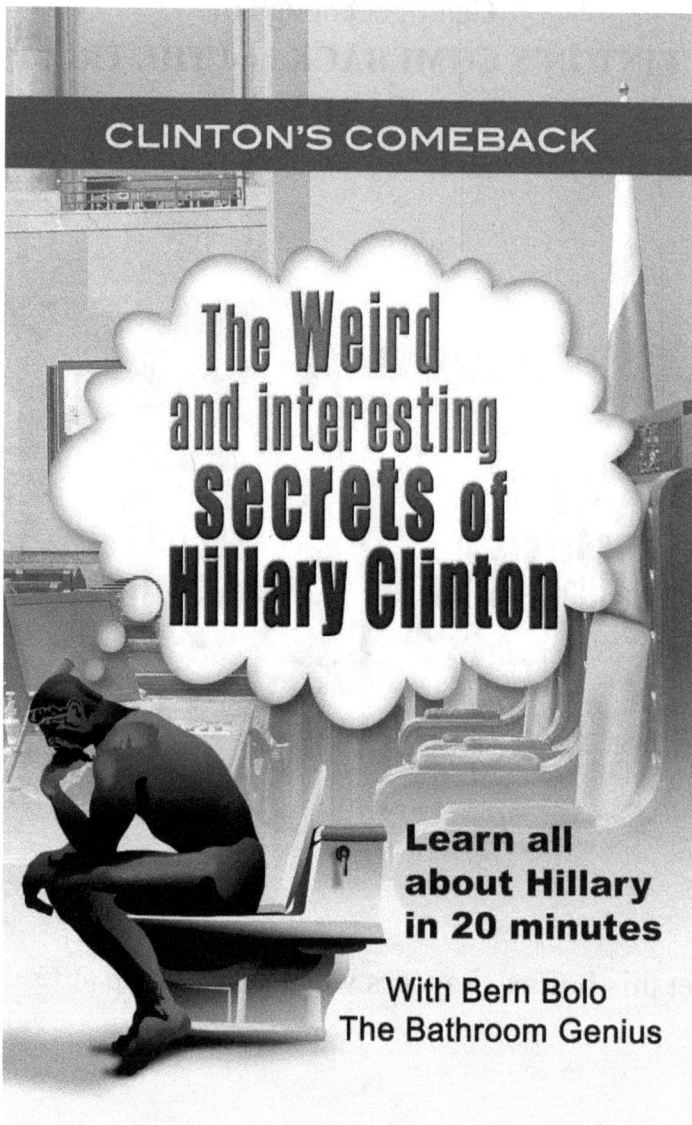

Every moment wasted looking back, keeps us from moving forward...In this world and the world of tomorrow, we must go forward together or not at all
–Hillary Clinton

After losing the 2008 nomination to Barrack Obama, she is now back to her aim of being the first female president of the United States.

Will she finally be successful the second time around?

Bern Bolo and J.J. Tocaldo's **CLINTON'S COMEBACK: WEIRD AND INTERESTING SECRETS OF HILLARY CLINTON** will help you know more about Hillary Clinton from her personality to her profession and her political philosophy and plans. It will also contain some interesting and weird facts of this presidential hopeful. The trivia book aims to help you and the rest of the voters of America to determine if Hillary Clinton deserves to become the leader of our great country.

A PREVIEW of WEIRD and INTERESTING SECRETS you can get from this trivia & facts book:
- How did she rise above her scandals and illegal activities.
- Weird and interesting facts about Hillary Clinton.
- What her secret plans for the country are.
- Know Hillary's successes.
- Know what she is fighting for.

Let *Bern Bolo and J.J. Tocaldo's* **CLINTON'S COMEBACK: WEIRD AND INTERESTING SECRETS OF HILLARY CLINTON** help you decide who to vote and trust with the leadership our beloved country, United States of America.

Will Hillary Clinton be your "champion?"

Look for <u>CLINTON'S COMEBACK: Weird and Interesting Secrets of Hillary Clinton</u> **On Amazon**

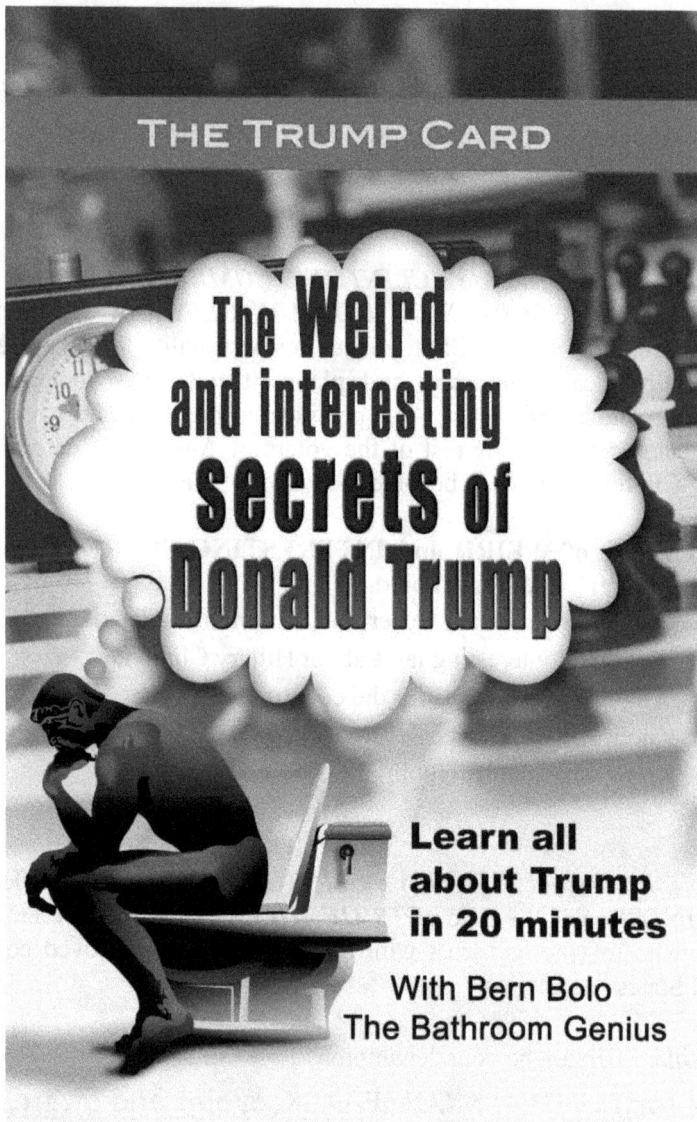

"I like thinking big. I always have. To me it's very simple: If you're going to be thinking anyway, you might as well think big."—Donald J. Trump

For this business mogul,

- Spending a million dollars is like you subscribing for a month of Netflix or buying a bottle of wine
- Spending $6 million on a mini mansion is like you buying a waffle maker
- Spending $43 million on a real mansion is like you buying the cheapest Apple watch

He's rich. He's successful. And under his leadership, the Trump empire has built a brand that is recognized worldwide. He pursues business ventures with a focus until he gets the results that he wants.

Now, he's in a new race, a contest that will take him straight to the White House in a new leadership position that can change the history of America.

Will he once again be able to succeed in this new endeavor of his?

*Bern Bolo and J.J. Tocaldo's **THE TRUMP CARD: WEIRD AND INTERESTING SECRETS OF DONALD TRUMP*** will help people know more about Donald Trump from his personality to his profession and his political philosophy and plans. It will also contain some interesting and weird facts of this presidential hopeful. The trivia book aims to help you and the rest of the voters of America to determine if Donald Trump is deserving to become the leader of this great country.

A PREVIEW of the WEIRD and INTERESTING FACTS you can get from this trivia book:

- His political standpoints and platform
- His response on important issues such as immigration
- His plans for the country and what he is fighting for

- TRUMP'S LIFE IN LOVE.
- His views in faith and religion
- His plans for the veterans and the military
- His controversies from alleged bankruptcy, his marriages and even issues on him having Narcissistic Personality Disorder
- How he runs his life and his businesses

Let *Bern Bolo and J.J. Tocaldo's* ***THE TRUMP CARD: WEIRD AND INTERESTING SECRETS OF DONALD TRUMP*** help you decide who to vote and trust with the leadership of the United States of America.

Exercise your right to suffrage and get to know your candidates. Go for the person which can spark positive changes in the country and the one who embodies the principles you believe in. Are you willing to join Trump in his quest to "Make America great again?" You count so make your vote count.

Look for THE TRUMP CARD: Weird and Interesting Secrets of Donald Trump On Amazon

About the Authors

Bern Bolo

For someone who, two years ago, did not even know how to copy-and-paste, I am very thankful to have come such a long way. I couldn't have guessed that my spirit was leading to business and entrepreneurship. It did not matter that I knew very little. I had the courage and the right drive and I knew that I was already halfway there.

It was through business books such as Zero to One, The One Minute Manager, Cashflow Quadrant and Unfair Advantage that I was able to get the necessary education that I needed to get me where I am today. Through them, I received epiphany after epiphany and now my dreams are a reality. Books are indeed one of the most powerful tools one can ever have.

Through my steadily growing business, I hope to provide inspiration and opportunity to people all over the globe. It is not impossible to reach your dreams too.

For my readers, may these books be able to open you to the immense possibilities that this world has to offer. Through my words, let your spirit wake up and allow it to guide you to your path towards success.

J. J. Tocaldo

J. J. Tocaldo is a reader, a writer, a storyteller and an adventurer. She loves a simple conversation between friends and a quiet day at home with her pen and amongst her books.

Although pursuing a career in health, she loves words just as much as she enjoys healing and being of service to others. She reads and writes as often as she can, in between work and the relentless barrage of requirements.

She believes in happy endings, hot chocolates in cold weather and in making the world a better place.

www.ingramcontent.com/pod-product-compliance
Lightning Source LLC
Chambersburg PA
CBHW060527280326
41933CB00014B/3110